ORCA
FOOTPRINTS

Down to Earth

HOW KIDS HELP FEED THE WORLD

NIKKI TATE

ORCA BOOK PUBLISHERS

Library and Archives Canada Cataloguing in Publication

Tate, Nikki, 1962-
Down to earth : how kids help feed the world / Nikki Tate.
(Footprints)

Includes bibliographical references and index.
Issued also in electronic formats.
ISBN 978-1-4598-0423-4

1. Agriculture--Developing countries--Juvenile literature.
2. Livestock--Developing countries--Juvenile literature. 3. Food supply--Developing countries--Juvenile literature. 4. Children--Juvenile literature. I. Title. II. Series: Footprints (Victoria, B.C.)

s519.T38 2013   j630   C2012-907694-5

First published in the United States, 2013
Library of Congress Control Number: 2012953461

Summary: How kids all over the world help produce the food we eat.

Orca Book Publishers is dedicated to preserving the environment and has printed this book on Forest Stewardship Council® certified paper.

Orca Book Publishers gratefully acknowledges the support for its publishing programs provided by the following agencies: the Government of Canada through the Canada Book Fund and the Canada Council for the Arts, and the Province of British Columbia through the BC Arts Council and the Book Publishing Tax Credit.

Front cover photos by Getty Images
Back cover photos (top left to right): Iman M.P. Hejiboer, Danielle Tate-Stratton, Nikki Tate; bottom left to right: Sustainable Harvest International, Terry Joyce, Adebayo O.T./Iita
Design by Teresa Bubela

ORCA BOOK PUBLISHERS
PO Box 5626, STN. B
Victoria, BC Canada
V8R 6S4

ORCA BOOK PUBLISHERS
PO Box 468
Custer, WA USA
98240-0468

www.orcabook.com
Printed and bound in Canada.

16 15 14 13 • 4 3 2 1

Herds of black and white Holstein dairy cows are a familiar sight across North America. KEN COLE/DREAMSTIME.COM

For all the young farmers of the world—
without you, mealtimes would be dull indeed.

Contents

Introduction 6

CHAPTER ONE: SEEDS AND PLANTS

Amazing Things in Tiny Packages 8

Giant Seeds with Many Uses 8

Small Seeds, Massive Pumpkins 9

Why Does Genetic Diversity Matter? 10

Planting Seeds Around the World 11

Plants But No Seeds 11

Not Everyone Has a Garden 12

Back to Basics: Staple Crops 12

What's With the Price Tag? 16

CHAPTER TWO: FEATHERED FRIENDS

Chickens 18

Ducks 22

Turkeys 23

Pigeons 24

What Do Egg Carton Labels Tell Us? 24

CHAPTER THREE:
MULTI-PURPOSE ANIMALS

Goats 26
Pigs 28
Cattle 30
Sheep 32
Saving Rare Breeds of Farm Animals 35

CHAPTER FOUR:
AT WORK ON THE FARM

Dogs—Not Just Pets 36
Guardian Geese 36
Home on the Range 38
Getting from Here to There 38
Animals in the Field 39
Worms at Work 41
Bees 41
To Market, To Market 42
Open for Business 42

Resources 44
Acknowledgments 45
Index 47

Introduction

Children pick fresh tomatoes at a farm in India.
NIKHIL GANGAVANE/DREAMSTIME.COM

A young child in this family of Romanian farmers uses a long stick to beat the top branches of plum trees. The ripe plums fall to the ground, where they are easily collected. CATALIN PETOLEA/DREAMSTIME.COM

On family farms around the world, children help grow food.

Many community-garden and urban-farming projects in cities and towns welcome families and children, and more and more schools are setting aside space for food gardens. Lots of families grow vegetables or keep a few chickens in the backyard. You don't need much room to grow good stuff to eat: a large pot on a balcony produces more tomatoes than you might think!

When my nieces and nephew come to visit me at Dark Creek Farm, one of their favorite things to do is help me prepare a meal made with food we have grown or raised ourselves. Depending on the season, we might dig up some potatoes and harvest beets, tomatoes, carrots or parsnips to serve along with pork chops from one of our pigs. Dessert might be delicious strawberries served with ice cream made from fresh goat milk, or a rich custard tart made with some of our duck eggs.

A child in Kenya milks the family goat. IMAN M.P. HEJIBOER

Even in the dead of winter, we enjoy food we've frozen, dried or preserved in jars. There's no doubt that fresh peas picked moments before they appear on the dinner table are extremely tasty, and, even more important, there's something deeply satisfying about helping produce the food you eat.

In *Down to Earth* we'll explore some of the many ways children help collect seeds, weed gardens, milk goats, herd ducks and more as they grow, harvest, prepare and distribute food.

At Dark Creek Farm we love our Muscovy ducks. Alexander makes friends with this duckling that will grow up to lay delicious eggs for us to eat.
DANIELLE TATE-STRATTON

CHAPTER ONE

Seeds and Plants

Seeds are packed with all the nutrients young plants need to start growing. TOM GISEL

Riddle: *Throw away the outside and cook the inside. Then eat the outside and throw away the inside. What did you just eat?*

Answer: *An ear of corn.*

AMAZING THINGS IN TINY PACKAGES

What do carrots, pumpkins and lettuce have in common? Yes, they are all things to eat, but they are also all easily grown from seeds. Whether a farmer plants a huge field of wheat or a family in an apartment nurtures salad greens in pots out on the balcony, it all begins with a handful of seeds.

GIANT SEEDS WITH MANY USES

Coconuts are some of the most useful seeds in the world. Not only can you eat the meat of a coconut (the white, fleshy part); you can also polish floors with the husk, cook with coconut milk and use coconut shells for fuel.

Children in the Solomon Islands climb palm trees to harvest coconuts. NADINE AU-YONG

FOOD FACT: Some seeds, like carrot seeds, are tiny. Twenty-four thousand carrot seeds only weigh about 28 grams (1 ounce)! Some are huge. The largest seed in the world is from the Coco de Mer, a kind of palm tree found in the Seychelles. These huge coconuts can be 30 centimeters (12 inches) long and weigh 24 kg (44 lbs)!

Even before plants send roots down in the soil and leaves up toward the sun, young sprouts provide nutritious snacks for people. Some kinds of routed seeds are particularly tasty. Mung bean sprouts are popular in stir-fries, alfalfa sprouts are great in sandwiches, and giant sunflower sprouts add a delicious crunch to salads. Check for sprouts in the salad area of the grocery store or try sprouting your own at home! AMANDA VALLOZA

SMALL SEEDS, MASSIVE PUMPKINS

You might be able to hold a whole lot of pumpkin seeds in your hand, but chances are you won't be able to budge the gigantic pumpkins that can be grown from these flat seeds.

Each year in the autumn, many rural communities host country fairs. Pumpkin-growing contests provide a challenge for gardeners of all ages, and the results make popular displays.

Roasted pumpkin seeds are a tasty snack! RACHEL TAYSE

The Delaney family of Pickering, Ontario (Chris, Jen, Alanna and Kirsten), worked together to grow this giant pumpkin, which won first prize at the 2012 Norfolk County Fair and Horse Show in Ontario and weighed in at a whopping 765 kg (1,683 lbs). JENNIFER SHAFTO

The largest seed bank in the world is the Millennium Seed Bank Project near London, England. A secure underground vault provides safe storage for billions of seed samples. The bank provides samples to researchers and seed banks elsewhere in the world, and it also conducts research on seeds included in the collection. WIKIPEDIA/PATCHE99Z

Carrots come in many sizes, shapes and colors.
TEXAS A&M AGRILIFE COMMUNICATIONS/
KATHLEEN PHILLIPS

FOOD FACT: In October 2011, the record for the world's largest pumpkin was awarded to Jim and Kelsey Bryson of Ormstown, Quebec. Their entry to the Prince Edward County Pumpkinfest weighed an astonishing 824.9 kg (1,818.5 lbs)! That's a lot of pumpkin pie!

WHY DOES GENETIC DIVERSITY MATTER?

Did you know there are about 5,000 varieties of potatoes? And yet, it's unusual to find more than a handful of types for sale. The varieties available in grocery stores tend to be uniform in size and shape, travel well and produce consistently good yields per acre. While these are all handy traits if you are interested in shipping potatoes that travel and store well, there are dangers associated with only producing certain types of any crop.

Each kind of potato (or apple or cucumber or corn—or any other type of crop you can imagine) is resistant to certain diseases and pests, prefers a slightly cooler or hotter temperature and damper or drier conditions, and is adapted to particular soil types and weather patterns. Each variety also looks and tastes slightly different. If farmers grow only one type of potato, these other traits are in danger of being lost. If a disease comes along that threatens a popular variety, it's important that we still have access to less popular options. They might be smaller or less productive varieties, but they might be resistant to that disease, which makes their genetics invaluable.

Small-scale farmers often grow unusual varieties and save and share seeds with other farmers in order to preserve the genetic material of less common types of food crops.

Several international initiatives preserve seeds on a large scale. At the Svalbard Global Seed Vault not far from the North Pole in Norway, seeds from all over the world are preserved in a specially designed underground cavern.

Site of the Svalbard Global Seed Vault, Norway. SVALBARD GLOBAL SEED VAULT/MARI TEFRE

PLANTING SEEDS AROUND THE WORLD

Sometimes volunteers travel to different parts of the world to help local farmers plant crops. These farms help feed local families and may also produce cash crops—crops that are grown to sell, sometimes to consumers on the other side of the globe. Products like coffee, chocolate and bananas may travel thousands of kilometers after they are harvested.

PLANTS BUT NO SEEDS

Not all plants are grown from seeds. In Hawaii, pineapple crowns are planted on the surface of the ground. A year-round growing season and copper-rich volcanic soil make places like Hawaii perfect for growing these tasty (if prickly!) fruits.

A volunteer with Sustainable Harvest International plants cucumber seeds with children in Honduras. SUSTAINABLE HARVEST INTERNATIONAL

On Dark Creek Farm

Dark Creek Farm is a very small farm, just under 1 hectare (2 acres) in size. Strawberries are really popular here, but we didn't have enough room to plant as many berries as we'd like. Our solution? Grow up! We grow our strawberries in fabric bags that hang from a rack. That way, we can grow more plants in less space—always a good thing around here! Though it is possible to grow strawberry plants from seeds, it's more common to use new young plants that develop from runners sent out from mature strawberry plants.

Strawberry racks make the most use of limited space. DANIELLE TATE-STRATTON

This community garden in Washington, DC, encourages garden lovers of all ages to work together to grow amazing food.
TED EYTAN, MD

FOOD FACT:
Every year, more than 600 million metric tons (about 661 million short tons) of wheat are produced around the world.

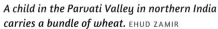

A child in the Parvati Valley in northern India carries a bundle of wheat. EHUD ZAMIR

NOT EVERYONE HAS A GARDEN

Lots of communities and schools have gardens that are shared by many people. Gardens like these are excellent for people who live in small apartments or who are learning about gardening.

BACK TO BASICS: STAPLE CROPS

People living in different parts of the world rely on different staple crops to provide a significant portion of their diets. These plants may be prepared and eaten in many ways. Various types of grains, for example, can be ground up to make flour, which can then be used to make porridge, crackers, pastry, bread and other foods that might be boiled, baked, fried or soaked before eating.

Wheat: What's in That Loaf of Bread?

Making bread from wheat hasn't changed much for centuries. Flour (made from ground-up wheat seeds), water, salt and a rising agent (yeast or baking soda) are mixed together before being cooked. Flatbreads like chapatis, naan and pita often omit the rising agent.

In Bangladesh, a type of flatbread called roti is a staple food. S. MOJUMDER/DRIK/CIMMYT

Corn

Corn (also called maize) has been cultivated for about 6,000 years and is still a staple crop in South America. Some varieties of corn are sweet and eaten like a vegetable. Other varieties are better suited to making cornmeal or corn flour. Popcorn is made by heating corn kernels with some cooking oil.

Corn is one of the most versatile crops grown anywhere. Dried corn kernels might be used to make tortilla chips, corn oil, animal feed or breakfast cereal. You'll find corn in some surprising places, including beer, chewing gum and ketchup. Nonedible items made with corn include crayons, chalk and soap.

This Himba boy in Namibia cooks corn (maize) for lunch. ALEXTARA/DREAMSTIME.COM

Before rice can be planted, the mud in the paddy fields must be softened. Children are given the responsibility of chasing oxen around with sticks to make them charge through the mud, trampling the ground in the process. LEE XIAN JIE

One way to grind sorghum into flour is to crush the kernels between two stones. This mother in the Lower Omo Valley in southwest Ethiopia is stone-grinding sorghum with her children. NGAIRE LAWSON

Rice

Though a great deal of wheat and corn is grown worldwide, much of it is used for animal feed. Globally, rice is the single most important food crop for people.

Rice plants thrive in flooded fields where weeds and pests do not grow well. China and India are the world's largest producers of rice.

Grinding Grains

It's easy to open a box of cereal and pour out the puffed wheat or crispy corn. That's because the wheat, corn or rice that went into making that cereal was harvested, husked and ground up at a factory before being processed into cereal. All you have to do is pour it in a bowl and add some milk!

In many countries, families grow their own staple crops. Grinding up these plants and grains so they can be cooked and eaten is a time-consuming task when it is done by hand, and children are often called upon to help.

In the savannah (dry grasslands) areas of Africa, staple crops like millet (a type of grain), sorghum (a type of wheat) and groundnuts (known as peanuts in North America) are grown both for local use and to export.

Groundnuts

Peanut butter is common in North America, but in places like Sub-Saharan Africa, groundnuts are made into a thick sauce. Poured over plantains (a type of banana) or rice, the sauce is a great source of oil and protein.

Mighty Soybeans

Soybeans were first cultivated in China about five thousand years ago and were traditionally considered one of the five sacred plants (along with rice, wheat, barley and millet). Today, soybeans (or soya beans) are grown all over the world, and products made from this handy crop include soy milk, tofu, soy flour and various imitation meat products that are used in processed vegetarian foods.

Celebrating the Yam

There's no question that food is tasty. But some kinds of food are so important to a culture that festivals and rituals celebrate their successful harvest. In Papua New Guinea, farming tribes like the Abelam depend on yams, taro and sweet potatoes to survive. Men compete to see who can grow the biggest yam each year, and the whole community celebrates the yam during an annual festival.

Cassava

Cassava is grown as a staple in many places in the world. Not only is this crop an important source of carbohydrates for more than 500 million people, it's also a good source of water. In the Amazon region of Colombia, water is extracted from a mash made from cassava roots.

> **FOOD FACT:** It's estimated that one fifth of the calories consumed by people around the world come from rice.

Children in the Sepik area of Papua New Guinea dress up to celebrate during the annual yam harvest. RITA WILLAERT

Cassava is a hardy crop that can grow in poor soil and without much water.
ADEBAYO O.T./IITA

Food like these bananas sometimes travels thousands of kilometers from the farm where it was grown to the grocery store in your neighborhood. Buying fruit labeled Organic or Fair Trade *can help ensure that farmers are paid a fair price for their produce.* FRANK JUHAS

Farms in the United States grow more soybeans than anywhere else in the world, though originally most US farmers only raised this crop to feed livestock. UPTALL/DREAMSTIME.COM

WHAT'S WITH THE PRICE TAG?

Why is it that a kilogram of organic carrots can cost so much more than a kilogram of regular carrots? Large-scale, non-organic farms that use chemicals to fertilize crops and control weeds, and lots of big equipment to harvest and process the food they produce, can keep their prices low. Large farms are also eligible for government grants and subsidies not available to small farms. Small, organic farms rely on more labor-intensive farming methods (for example, picking caterpillars off fruit trees by hand rather than spraying with a chemical pesticide). It takes more time to collect and dig in animal manure and compost to improve the soil than it does to spray on a chemical fertilizer. These less-efficient methods drive costs up. Though growing crops using chemical assistance can produce higher yields, doing so often has other environmental costs that are not passed on directly to the consumer—at least, not in the price paid at the checkout counter. Soil quality declines if it isn't built up by adding compost. Toxins can build up in the environment. Beneficial insects can be killed by pesticides intended to control pests. And those same pests can develop resistance to chemicals, which in turn leads to the use of harsher chemicals. Nobody is sure of the long-term environmental and health effects of chemical use in agriculture. Supporters of organic farming suggest that, in the long run, foods grown more naturally are better for all of us—and our farms—and are worth extra production costs.

Pineapples take about eighteen months to reach maturity. ELSIE HUI

CHAPTER TWO

Feathered Friends

Riddle: *If apples come from an apple tree, what kind of tree do chickens come from?*

Answer: *A poul-tree.*

CHICKENS

For centuries, chickens have lived alongside people, gobbling up our leftovers and spilled grain in exchange for providing eggs and the occasional chicken dinner. Today's chickens descend from a couple of types of wild jungle fowl found in southeast Asia. They come in all shapes, sizes, colors and hairstyles, and they are the most plentiful species of domestic bird on the planet. One estimate puts the number of chickens at more than 24 billion. That's a lot of eggs and drumsticks!

Keeping Chickens is Easy

Many communities in North America allow households to keep a few chickens in the backyard. The rules vary from town to town, so before you rush out to a farm to buy chickens, be sure to check the local regulations! Chicken accommodation can be simple or fancy, but it must be secure so hens are protected from predators at night. Even in the city, raccoons, cats and dogs can be dangerous to chickens.

In some places, chickens run wild. For some very poor families, collecting eggs or occasionally catching one of these feral birds provides a welcome source of food.

Chickens come in all shapes and sizes. Some are bred for a particular type of feather, others for the color of their eggs and others for their size and meat. CREATED BY L. PRANG & CO.

Children are often responsible for feeding the chickens and collecting eggs. JOSEPH W. NIENSTEDT

On Dark Creek Farm

We move this small chicken coop to different areas of the farm. Surrounded by portable electric fencing, our chickens can eat grass and scratch for worms and grubs without roaming away. At night, the chickens sleep on a perch in the coop. They lay their eggs in nesting boxes inside their portable house.

DANIELLE TATE-STRATTON

There are more chickens on the planet than people! This boy and chicken live in Sri Lanka. JOYFULL/DREAMSTIME.COM

4-H and 4-H related programs exist in more than 80 countries around the world.

REGISTERED TRADEMARK OF THE CANADIAN 4-H COUNCIL

4-H for Serious Young Farmers

The four *H*s in the 4-H clover represent the words *hands, health, heart* and *head.* The words come from the 4-H pledge:

> *I pledge my Head to clearer thinking,*
> *my Heart to greater loyalty,*
> *my Hands to larger service,*
> *and my Health to better living for my club, my community,*
> *my country and my world.*

Children who get involved in the 4-H program can choose from many clubs within it. Many groups involve some aspect of farming and are organized for those interested in raising chickens, horses, swine, beef and rabbits. There are also 4-H clubs for activities like gardening, technology, photography and community service. In all cases, the emphasis is on learning by doing. Children who participate in a 4-H poultry club might raise poultry to produce eggs or meat. Keeping careful records, making presentations, creating educational displays and competing at local country fairs are all activities poultry-club members might try.

Showing farm animals at the local fair each fall is one of the highlights of the year for 4-H participants like Maddy from Vancouver Island in British Columbia, Canada. In this showmanship class, she must show off the best features of her pig to the judge.
DANIELLE TATE-STRATTON

CHICKEN FACTS

- ★ Chickens don't have teeth. They need access to grit (very fine gravel or sand), which they use in their gizzards to grind up the food they eat.
- ★ The chicken is the closest living relative to *Tyrannosaurus rex*.
- ★ If you are terrified of chickens, you're an alektorophobe.
- ★ The record for the largest number of yolks in a single egg is nine!
- ★ Chicken eggs are usually white or brown but can also be blue or green.
- ★ A good laying hen will produce about 300 eggs per year.

FOOD FACT: Did you know you can eat ostrich meat? One adult ostrich yields about 59 kg (130 lbs) of meat.

The red, fleshy part on a Muscovy duck's head is called a caruncle. MACIEJ SWIC/DREAMSTIME.COM

DUCKS

If you live near a park with a pond, you have probably seen ducks paddling around. But did you know that ducks are popular birds to raise on farms? Not only are many duck breeds good sources of meat, but their eggs are also delicious.

Most domestic duck breeds descend from wild mallard ducks. An exception is the Muscovy duck, a breed some people feel is actually more closely related to geese. Muscovy ducks are quackless, make great mothers, love eating slugs and other garden pests, and lay big eggs.

On Dark Creek Farm

Aly spends most of her summer holidays at Dark Creek Farm. One of her jobs is to collect duck eggs. Some of the eggs are sold at our farm stand, and others wind up in baked goods, omelets and other tasty treats. Each day Aly selects the best-looking egg and sets it aside. She carefully collects eggs that have consistent markings (some Muscovy duck eggs have pale green spots at one end, and others are plain) and are the same size, shape and color. By the time the fall fair rolls around, she has a perfectly matched set of six eggs to enter in the fair. Aly has won lovely ribbons for having the best egg display at the fair!

Aly with her prize-winning Dark Creek Farm duck eggs. NIKKI TATE

TURKEYS

For many families, traditional holiday dinners wouldn't be complete without a roast turkey.

In the wild (or on farms that raise heritage breeds of turkeys), a hen lays a dozen or so eggs, at the rate of about one per day. She then sits on her nest for twenty-eight days, until the young turkeys (poults) hatch. Though turkey eggs are a bit bigger than chicken eggs and are very good to eat, most turkeys in North America are raised for their meat, which is usually eaten for Christmas or Thanksgiving.

Like other varieties of poultry, turkeys need a secure place to roost at night and daily feeding and watering. Clean, dry bedding is essential for keeping turkeys healthy. Cleaning out the turkey house isn't the most pleasant of jobs, but it's absolutely necessary to keep turkeys happy and help them thrive. Turkeys love to roam and do well on pasture during the day. They eat grass, berries, seeds, grubs and worms. Despite their size, turkeys fly well and like to roost in trees. It's a good idea to herd turkeys into their shelter before dusk or it's hard to convince them to come down out of the trees!

Marius herds the Dark Creek turkeys into their house at night. The long sticks are used to guide the turkeys, never to hit them!
DANIELLE TATE-STRATTON

On Dark Creek Farm

When people come to visit Dark Creek Farm, they say two things about our turkeys: "They're so big!" and "They look so weird!" The fleshy bit that dangles down over a turkey's beak is called a snood. Both males (called gobblers or toms) and females (hens) have snoods and wattles (the flap of skin under the chin).

Turkey snoods can change color! A relaxed tom turkey's snood is bright red. When he gets agitated, it turns blue. MARIUS CALIN

This rooftop pigeon coop is located in New York City. Some pigeons are raised for meat, others for racing and still others as fancy show birds. STÉPHANE MISSIER

PIGEONS

Turkeys, ostriches, emus and even chickens are all good-sized birds that provide many pounds of delicious meat. Pigeons, on the other hand, are much smaller, but they also can be raised to eat. They can be kept in much smaller spaces than their larger relatives and are sometimes found in rooftop coops right in the middle of the city.

WHAT DO EGG CARTON LABELS TELL US?

Next time you are shopping for eggs, have a close look at the labels on the cartons. What do they mean, anyway? Eggs from conventional, large-scale poultry farms are laid by hens that live in small cages (called battery cages) inside huge enclosed buildings. Thousands of chickens live in close quarters and are fed carefully designed feeds that provide all their nutritional needs but might also include medications, supplements or genetically modified grains.

Animal Welfare Approved

This designation is given to family farms that raise chickens in the most humane manner possible. Farms participating in this program must raise their chickens outdoors on pasture and follow strict rules regarding space, housing, feed, medication and handling. Farms must agree to be inspected.

Organic

Eggs labeled *Organic* come from chickens that must eat feed free of antibiotics, chemical pesticides, herbicides, fertilizers and genetically modified grains. Organically raised chickens must be uncaged and have access to an outdoor run. The law does not require the run to contain any grass or bugs, and if many chickens use a smallish outdoor area, it doesn't take long for them to turn it into a barren patch of dirt.

Free Range

Free-range eggs come from chickens that must have access to the outdoors, though they don't necessarily receive organic food or have the chance to roam over large areas to find their own food. Pasture-raised birds eat grass, bugs and other goodies they find for themselves and generally receive supplementary feed, which may or may not be organically produced.

Sadly, even though consumers like the idea of supporting farmers who raise chickens in the most humane way possible, there are no official standards for the words used on egg cartons, and therefore no real way to verify whether statements made on labels actually reflect conditions on farms.

So how do you know just what kind of life the chicken that laid the eggs your family ate for breakfast has led? The best way to find out is to visit the farm your eggs come from. Or get to know the farmer who brings the eggs to the local farmers' market. Of course, if your city permits backyard coops, you can keep a few hens and let them produce eggs for your family.

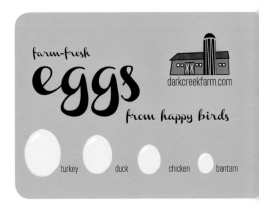

Would you buy eggs labeled like this? What does the phrase "from happy birds" mean to you? What other information would you like to see on this label?
DANIELLE TATE-STRATTON

FOOD FACT: Chicken and turkey are two commonly eaten kinds of poultry, but specialty farms also raise ducks, geese, guinea fowl, pheasants, ostrich, emu, quail and peacocks for the dinner table.

CHAPTER THREE

Multi-Purpose Animals

Keeping domestic animals is not a new idea. Ancient Egyptians enjoyed milk just as much as we do! DAVE ELSWORTH/ILRI

Large, specialized farms may only have one breed of farm animal, but on many smaller farms you'll still find a collection of animals, each of which might be used in several ways. Goats, sheep, cows and pigs are all versatile animals that contribute to farm life in various ways.

GOATS

Goats are useful for many reasons: they produce milk, meat and fiber. Their quirky personalities, curiosity and friendliness toward people also mean they make great pets. Small enough to be controlled by children but strong enough to pull a fair amount of weight, goats were often seen hitched to small carts in the past. It's less common today, but goats are still used as draft animals.

FOOD FACT:
Bovine refers to cattle
Ovine refers to sheep
Swine refers to pigs
Caprine refers to goats

A Masai child milks a goat. Milk doesn't get much fresher than this! KEITH MARRAN

Goat Milk

Fresh goat milk is delicious and nutritious. It's also versatile. Cheese, yogurt and ice cream can all be made quite easily with goat milk. For some people with dairy allergies, goat milk is a little less irritating than milk from cows.

The Datooga people of Tanzania raise goats for meat and milk. NGAIRE LAWSON

On Dark Creek Farm

Poppy is a resident milk goat at Dark Creek Farm. This white farm cheddar is made from Poppy's milk.

DANIELLE TATE-STRATTON

This child in Mozambique keeps an eye on his grazing goat. ANDREW WINEARLS

Like all farm animals, goats need access to fresh drinking water, good food and shelter from rain and wind. Goats like to climb and appreciate having places that will get them off the ground. Sleeping platforms are often found in goat shelters. Goats are amazing escape artists—they can leap, climb and scramble over and under all kinds of obstacles—so good fencing is needed to keep them in designated pastures and out of vegetable gardens.

Goats are actually quite finicky eaters—they don't really eat tin cans! They do enjoy browsing on small bushes, they love eating brambles, and they have been known to scramble up into trees to get at fresh, tasty leaves.

PIGS

Pigs come in many shapes and sizes, from the relatively small miniature breeds to giants like the English breed known as the Large Black Hog.

A sow (adult female pig) has an average of ten piglets per litter after a pregnancy that lasts about three months, three weeks and three days. Raised on pasture, the piglets take six to eight months to reach a suitable size for slaughter (about 90 to 100 kilograms or 200 to 225 pounds).

Pigs enjoy eating a wide range of foods and appreciate being fed table scraps (though it's best not to feed them meat). They get quite excited when they catch sight of the slop bucket (the pail where food scraps are collected in the kitchen). Pigs can move pretty fast, even when they get quite large.

PIG FACTS:

Everybody knows sausages, bacon, ham, pork roasts and chops come from pigs, but did you know you can make all of the following from them as well?

PRODUCT	PART OF PIG USED
Footballs and gloves	Fine leather from skin
Buttons	Bone
Hairbrushes	Bristles and hair
Jewelry	Teeth
Soap	Fat/lard

FOOD FACT: Large Black Hogs can grow to weigh more than 725 kg (1,600 lbs). That could feed a whole lot of people bacon for breakfast!

Maddy spends a little time with one of the Large Black Hogs at Dark Creek Farm.
DANIELLE TATE-STRATTON

On Dark Creek Farm

As a member of the 4-H Beef and Swine Club, Maddy will raise a piglet, feeding it and taking care of it until it is sold at auction at the local country fair in the autumn. As part of her swine project, Maddy will measure and record how much food Mawii eats and how much weight she gains.

Maddy and her piglet, Mawii.
DANIELLE TATE-STRATTON

It's unusual to see a sow with a single piglet. The average litter has ten piglets.
KABSIK PARK

Children in the Dominican Republic milk the family cow. Any extra milk and cheese not needed by the family is sold to local buyers.
MERCEDES RAMIREZ GUERRERO

Pigs make lots of interesting noises. Grunts, mumbles, sighs and even a noise that sounds a bit like chirping are all ways pigs communicate with each other and their human caretakers. A pig that's frightened or in pain makes an incredibly loud squealing noise. Loud noises are measured in decibels. A screaming pig (115 decibels) is actually louder than a jet engine taking off (113 decibels)! This is why people who work with pigs wear earplugs when they have to do something the pigs don't like.

CATTLE

It's estimated that there are more than 1.5 billion cattle in the world. Though beef is a popular kind of meat enjoyed by millions of people, it isn't the most efficient way to get calories from food. It takes several kilograms of grain- or corn-based feed to produce one kilogram of meat. Switching to a diet that includes more grains, legumes and vegetables and smaller portions of meat is not only healthy; it's also a little easier on the environment, as less land is needed for grazing and for grain and hay production.

This boy and his mother in southern Ethiopia milk their cow. EDWARDJE/DREAMSTIME.COM

These cattle are from the Calvert Hills Cattle Ranch in the Northern Territory of Australia. ANDY HILL

More Milk!

The family cow was once a standard feature on the family farm, and in many places in the world, cows are still milked by hand.

Generally, dairies keep many cows, and all the milk is collected in large storage tanks. This milk is then taken to processing facilities, where it is turned into a wide range of dairy products, such as yogurt, butter and hard and soft cheeses.

Whether a family keeps a single cow or a huge dairy operation maintains a big herd, dairy cows must be milked twice a day, every single day. In larger commercial dairies, milking machines are able to handle large volumes of milk quickly and efficiently.

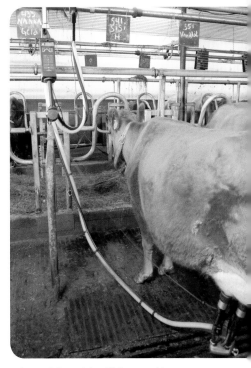

A large dairy with milking machines can milk many cows at the same time.
DANIELLE TATE-STRATTON

FOOD FACT: It takes almost 4 liters (about a gallon) of milk to make 500 grams (just over a pound) of hard cheese (a bit less to make soft cheese), so it's a good thing a cow produces plenty.

A little boy looks over a flock of sheep with his father and uncle in Kyrgyzstan. EVGENI ZOTOV

SHEEP

Used for their wool, meat and milk, sheep have been domesticated for more than ten thousand years.

Though many domestic animals produce fiber (llamas, alpacas, goats, rabbits and even dogs), sheep wool is still the most popular.

A boy in Romania with his flock of sheep. CARANICA NICOLAE/DREAMSTIME.COM

SHEEP FACTS:

Did you know that you can milk a sheep? A ewe (female sheep) is obviously a lot smaller than a cow and doesn't produce nearly as much milk each day, but milk from sheep is richer and creamier, which makes it perfect for cheese-making. Farmers in many countries carefully collect milk from ewes and then make fancy cheeses like these.

COUNTRY	TYPE OF CHEESE
Greece	Feta
France	Roquefort
Italy	Ricotta, Pecorino, Romano, Pecorino Sardo
Spain	Manchego

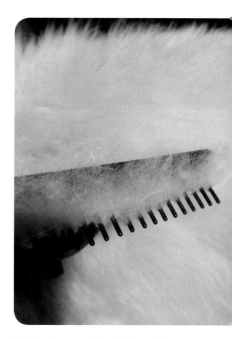

Unlike sheep wool, which must be sheared, the soft goat fiber known as cashmere must be combed out each spring. NIKKI TATE

33

Feeding a lamb milk from a bottle. DAN BAILLIE/BAILLIE PHOTOGRAPHY

Lambing Season

Many farm animals give birth in the springtime, when the weather is warm and the grasses are starting to grow. Sheep are no exception. When a farmer keeps a large flock of sheep, many ewes have their lambs at about the same time. This can mean many sleepless nights for farmers while they keep an eye on the pregnant ewes. Usually the lambs arrive just fine, but occasionally something goes wrong and a lamb is orphaned. In cases like this, the lamb must be fed from a bottle until it is old enough to eat grass and grain.

FOOD FACT: *Lamb* refers to meat from a young sheep in its first year. *Hogget* comes from a sheep between about 9 and 18 months old, and *mutton* is meat from an adult sheep.

SAVING RARE BREEDS OF FARM ANIMALS

In the same way that it's important to maintain the genetic diversity of food crops, it's just as important to preserve diversity in farm-animal genetics. Much of this work is being done by small-scale farmers who breed heritage varieties of livestock. Though these animals may not produce as many eggs or liters of milk or kilograms of meat in a year, their genetics provide valuable variations in taste, quality, disease resistance and adaptation to regional conditions. These qualities, as long as they are being maintained in viable breeding populations, can then be used by larger commercial operations to improve the overall health and productivity of their animals by occasionally crossbreeding their stock with these traditional breeds.

Organizations like the American Livestock Breeds Conservancy and Rare Breeds Canada provide information, education and support for farmers interested in raising heritage breeds of livestock. THE AMERICAN LIVESTOCK BREEDS CONSERVANCY

The woolly Mangalitsa pig was once common in Hungary. A handful of farmers has started to breed these rare pigs to try to save them from extinction. NIKKI TATE

FOOD FACT: Sheep and goats are closely related, but you can tell them apart if you know what to look for. Goats have beards and divided upper lips. At the other end, goat tails stick up while sheep tails hang down. Goats prefer to nibble and browse on bushes, and sheep prefer to graze on grass.

Sheep know there is safety in numbers and stick close together in a flock, which means that with practice, one person can move sheep from one place to another.

At Work On The Farm

Riddle: **Why was the sheep arrested on the freeway?**

Answer: *For doing an illegal ewe-turn.*

This young border collie practices herding skills on a group of ducks. SALLY WALLIS/DREAMSTIME.COM

The Karakachan dog is an ancient breed still used today to guard livestock in Bulgaria. DENISE TAYLOR, EDUCATION 4 CONSERVATION

Farm animals don't just provide food and other useful products like wool. They also work hard to keep farms running. Children, too, are responsible for many of the jobs that need to be done around the farm. Sometimes, animals and children work together to help get everything done.

DOGS—NOT JUST PETS

On some farms, well-trained herding dogs help farmers manage even very large flocks. The shepherd communicates with the dogs using a series of whistles and voice commands.

Dogs are also used on farms to protect livestock. Some breeds live out in the fields with the animals they protect.

GUARDIAN GEESE

A barking dog is probably the first thing you think of when you consider what kinds of animals could guard a farm. But dogs aren't the only ones who will raise a ruckus and chase off an intruder.

A guard goose is more intimidating than you might think! TERRY JOYCE

Donkeys and llamas will also fiercely defend other members of the flock, even when the flock is made up of sheep, pigs or goats. And believe it or not, geese are excellent at patrolling the farm. They not only make noise when a stranger sets foot on the property but will also chase and peck at people they don't know. A hard goose bite feels like a sharp punch and can leave quite a bruise.

For the families who own them, geese are friendly birds that do a great job of keeping pests like slugs under control. Some farms and wineries use geese as pest controllers on a large scale. Geese also lay tasty eggs, provide lovely soft feathers—their fine, downy under-feathers were once commonly used to stuff pillows and comforters—and make delicious roast dinners for special occasions.

Handy helpers, geese control pests, eat grass and chase intruders. COURTESY OF THE CORTES DE CIMA WINERY

Horses move among the animals without frightening them and can work all day without running out of gas. Perhaps the best part of working with a horse rather than a piece of equipment is that a horse is good company and seems to enjoy listening to a rider's chatter during a long day out on the range. JEFF MARCUS/WHITE LIGHT PHOTOGRAPHY

HOME ON THE RANGE

Grazing animals need lots of room to roam. But keeping track of cattle, sheep and other livestock when they are spread out over hundreds or even thousands of hectares is quite a project. Moving animals from one grazing area to another helps keep pastureland in good shape.

Whether herding cattle on a ranch in Hawaii or sheep on large ranges in New Zealand or Australia, the horse is still one of the best tools a cowboy has to safely move herds from one place to another. Horses are agile and get into places inaccessible to ATVs.

Moving large herds of cattle from grazing areas to auction yards or winter pasture is a huge operation. Even today, when it comes time to move the cattle, everyone lends a hand to get the job done.

In Thailand, water buffalos move people from one place to another. JONATHAN PIO

GETTING FROM HERE TO THERE

In some rural communities, animals are more common than cars and trucks as a means of transportation.

A team of horses pulls a huge load of hay (dried grass). Stored in a dry barn, hay can feed grazing animals during long, cold winters when there's no grass to be found outside. REBECCA JAMES

ANIMALS IN THE FIELD

Producing crops is a long, slow process that can take a lot of labor. Fortunately, animal helpers can make the job go a little more smoothly. Hogs can be used to turn over the soil in a field that has not yet been planted. Their big noses are incredibly strong, and their instinct to root around in the dirt can be put to good use on the farm. Chickens are also excellent workers when it comes to turning over soil, as they scratch around in the dirt looking for insects and grubs to eat. Goats are useful for clearing land covered in brush, and geese and ducks are invaluable for removing slugs and caterpillars that might damage crops.

For shifting really heavy loads, nothing beats an elephant! FRANK JUHAS

On Dark Creek Farm

Muscovy ducks hunt for slugs and caterpillars in newly prepared vegetable beds. Later in the season, after the new vegetable plants are well established, the ducks will pay another visit to the garden to eat more pests. One theory about how Muscovy ducks got their name relates to the food they eat: mosquitos are one of their favorite treats.

NIKKI TATE

39

In El Salvador, oxen power a mill that grinds sugarcane to produce caldo de cana, or sugarcane juice. The juice is then processed into candy or syrup. LEE SHAVER

Water buffalo in Sri Lanka plow a rice paddy.
PAUL COWAN/DREAMSTIME.COM

Time to Plow

Before fields can be planted, farmers turn over the soil using a plow. For centuries, horses and oxen have helped with this job. Though in many places tractors have taken the place of farm animals, these strong animals still work with farmers to till the soil in preparation for planting.

Time to Harvest

When crops are ready to harvest, draft animals are once again harnessed and put to work.

Time to Grind

After the harvest, the tedious job of grinding crops can be helped along by using animal power.

WORMS AT WORK

When you think about farm animals, you probably think about chickens, cows and pigs. But what about worms? Worm farmers keep worms like red wigglers in big bins where the worms earn their keep by eating all kinds of waste. Food scraps, dead leaves, animal manure, coffee grounds and shredded newspaper make worms like these very happy.

In return for having all that great food delivered to their bins, the worms produce castings—worm poop! Said to be some of the best natural fertilizer to be found anywhere, worm droppings are put back into the fields or packaged in bags and sold to gardeners. Worms might not be the cuddliest farm animals around, but they win the prize for being the quietest!

BEES

Like worms, bees may be small but they make a mighty big contribution to the farm. Many plants need to be pollinated in order to produce fruit. Bees carry pollen from one plant to another, ensuring a good crop as they go. As a bonus, back in their hives they turn that pollen into honey, which is collected at the end of the growing season.

Bee suits allow beekeepers to work safely with bees. EDWARD J. BOCK/DREAMSTIME.COM

On Dark Creek Farm

Worm bins like these provide rich compost for the vegetable beds on Dark Creek Farm.

NIKKI TATE

Goods travel to market in Algeria on camel trains like these. Camels' wide, flat feet enable them to travel across the sand. Their ability to go long distances between drinks comes in handy when water is hard to find.
RAMZI MOHAMED MESSAI

This roadside stand in India sells gingerroot.
FRANK JUHAS

TO MARKET, TO MARKET

Growing food is one huge job for farm families. But just as important is the work of getting food to consumers. In some places, people buy their food at big grocery stores. In other places, farm stands at the side of the road sell fresh produce grown close by. Sometimes farmers must take their products to markets farther away.

OPEN FOR BUSINESS

Vegetables, fruit, berries and eggs are popular items at local markets. But there are also lots of other products available. Children help make jams, jellies, soaps and other products from the farm. Children not only help make some of these things but also, in some cases, take their turn chatting with customers at farm stands and farmers' markets, selling the goods produced on their farms. Most communities have farmers' markets, and some of those markets invite children to sell things they have made.

In some cases, the products at markets are handicrafts that can be made by anyone, not just someone who lives on a farm. If you like to make things, check with your local farmers' market to see if you are allowed to set up a table. Not only will you make a bit of pocket money, but you'll also meet some new friends at the market.

After all the hard work of growing tasty food, there's nothing more fun than sharing the harvest with friends!

Maddy on duty at the Alderley Grange, the farm stand where Dark Creek Farm sells its extra produce. DANIELLE TATE-STRATTON

Resources

Books

Bucklin-Sporer, Arden. *How to Grow a School Garden: A Complete Guide for Parents and Teachers.* Portland, OR: Timber Press, 2010.

Grant, Amanda. *Grow It, Cook It with Kids.* London, UK: Ryland Peters & Small, 2010.

Lovejoy, Sharon. *Roots, Shoots, Buckets & Boots: Activities To Do in the Garden.* New York, NY: Workman Publishing, 1999.

Rosen, Michael J. *Our Farm: Four Seasons with Five Kids on One Family's Farm.* Plain City, OH: Darby Creek Publishing, 2008.

Websites

4-H: http://www.4-h.org/

American Livestock Breeds Conservancy (ALBC): http://albc-usa.org/

Dark Creek Farm: http://www.darkcreekfarm.com

National FFA Organization (formerly Future Farmers of America): https://www.ffa.org

Seed Savers Exchange: http://www.seedsavers.org

Acknowledgments

As always, a veritable army of people helped make this book possible. The team at Orca was fabulous as this book grew from the seed of an idea into a book in full bloom. My editor, Sarah Harvey, was a delight to work with. My able assistant, Dani Tate-Stratton, put her nose to the grindstone and kept it there until every last image to be used in the book was present and accounted for. Few people will know just how grateful I am that I didn't have to deal with all of that. This book would not be what it is without the generous contributions of photographers from all over the world.

Writing a book is quite a challenging project, but running a farm is even harder—or easier, depending on the kind of day I'm having. I have never had as much fun, eaten as well or met as many great people as I have since my farm went from being a lovely hobby to an actual working farm capable of feeding many families. Thanks to all the farmers who have been so generous with advice and encouragement and also to all of you who have helped here on the farm, building fences, painting buildings, feeding the animals, milking the goat, collecting the eggs and trying to save the lives of my delicate turkeys. We would not have had strawberries without those cool hanging planters (thanks, Dani and Toryn!), huge squash and fabulous tomatoes without the new raised beds (thanks, Jonathan and Ally!), ducklings without the overhead netting over the new duck pens (yay Valerie and Frederic!) or vegetables without the most amazing weeder of all time (that would be you, Will!). Huge thanks as well to Maddy and Carol, goat muckers par excellence; Andrei and Vina, whose fields feed the lambs; Marilyn, who pastures the horses and chickens; Chloe and Andrew, who do all the truly terrible jobs with a big smile; Liz, who works from dawn to dusk and then shares the bounty; Colin, who can build anything and happily does so—how would I manage without all of you wonderful helpers? Without your efforts, the farm—and therefore this book—would not be possible. And, finally, thanks to all the children, relatives, friends and neighbors who come out to the farm and find such joy! Your delight in the farm and all that we grow here makes me so happy. Thank you!

There's nothing like the taste of sweet sap straight out of the tree! EILEEN KENNEDY-WARRINGTON

Index

Page numbers in **bold** indicate an image; there may also be text related to the same topic on that page

4-H, 20–21: pigs, 29

Africa, 14, 15
alpacas, 32
American Livestock Breeds Conservancy, 35
animal helpers, 36–41

backyard or balcony farms, 6, 8, 18, 25
bananas, 11, **16**. *See also* plantains
barley, 15
battery cages, 24
bees, **41**
border collies, **36**
bread, 12, **13**
Bryson, Jim and Kelsey, 10

camels, **42**
carrots, **10**: seeds, 8
cash crops, 11
cashmere, **33**
cassava, **15**
cattle, **2–3**, **30–31**: herding, 38; milking, **30**, **31**
cereal, 13, 14
cheese, 31: goat, **27**; sheep, 33
chickens, 6, **18–19**, **20**, 21, 24, 39: living conditions, 18, 19, 24–25
children: harvesting food, 6, **8**, 22; making farm products, 42; milking, 7, **27**, **30**; planting food, **11**, **14**; preparing food, 13, 14, **40**; raising animals, **21**, **29**, **34**; selling goods, 42, **43**; tending animals, **19**, **20**, **23**, **28**, **29**, **33**, **34**; work on farms, 6, 7, **12**, 36. *See also* 4-H; country fairs
China, 14, 15
chocolate, 11

Coco de Mer, 8
coconuts, **8**
coffee, 11
Colombia, 15
community gardens, 6, **12**
compost, 16, **41**
corn, **13**, 14: for livestock, 14, 30
country fairs, **9**, **21**, **22**, 29

dairy products, **27**, 31. *See also* cheese; milk
Dark Creek Farm, 6, 7, 11: chickens, **19**; eggs, **22**; goats, 27; Muscovy ducks, 7, 22, **39**; pigs, **29**; selling produce, 22, **43**; strawberries, **11**; turkeys, **23**; worms, 41
Delaney family, **9**
dogs, 32, **36**
donkeys, 37
ducks, 22, **36**, **39**. *See also* Muscovy ducks

eggs: chicken, 19, 21; duck, **22**; geese, 37; labels on cartons, 24–**25**; turkey, 23
elephants, **39**
emus, 24

farm stands, 22, **42**, **43**
farmers' markets, 25, 42
farming: 4-H clubs, **20–21**; backyard or balcony, 6, 8, 18, 25; chemical use, 16 (*see also* pest control); chickens, 24–25; children, 6–7, 36 (*see also* children); dairy, **31**; genetic diversity, 10–11, 35; harvesting food, **6**, **8**, 16, 40; large-scale vs small-scale, 16, 24–25, 26;

planting food, 8, 11, 39, **40** (*see also* seeds); processing food, 12, 13, 14, **14**, 15, 16, **40**; selling food, 11, 16, 22, 24–25, 30, 42, **42**, **43**; sharing seeds, 10; small-scale, 6, 10 (*see also* organic foods); urban, 6, 8, **12**, 18, 25; volunteers, 11. *See also* Dark Creek Farm
fertilizer, 16, 41
festivals, **15**. *See also* country fairs
flatbreads, 12, **13**
flour, 12, 13, **14**, 15
free-range, 25

gardens, 6, **12**
geese, 22, 37, 39
genetic diversity, 10–11, 35
goats, 26, **27**, **28**, 35, 39: housing, 28; milking, 7, **27**; fiber, 26, 32, **33**
grain, 12: for cattle feed, 30; for human diet, 14, 30; processing, **14**, 40. *See also* barley, corn, groundnuts, millet, rice, sorghum, soybeans, wheat
groundnuts, 14, 15
guard animals, 36–37

Hawaii, 11
hay, 39
herding, **23**, **36**, 38
hogget, 34. *See also* sheep
hogs. *See* pigs
honey, 41
horses, **38**, **39**, 40
housing. *See under* livestock; poultry

Index (continued)

India, 14

Karakachan dog, **36**

lamb, **34**. *See also* sheep
Large Black Hogs, 28, **29**
livestock, 26, 36: adjectives
   referring to, 26; feed for, 14, **16**,
   28, 30, 39; heritage varieties,
   35; housing, 28. *See also* alpacas;
   cattle; donkeys; goats; horses;
   llamas; oxen; pigs; rabbits;
   sheep; water buffalo
llamas, 32, 37

maize. *See* corn
Mangalitsa pig, **35**
markets, 42
meat: beef, 30; coconut, 8; goats,
   26; imitation, 15; pigs, 28;
   poultry, 18, 21, 22, 23, 24; sheep,
   32, 34
milk, 26: cattle, **30**, **31**; coconut, 8;
   goat, 7, **27**; sheep, 33; soy, 15
Millennium Seed Bank Project, **10**
millet, 14, 15
Muscovy ducks, 7, **22**, **39**: eggs, 22
mutton, 34. *See also* sheep
Norway, **11**

organic foods: eggs, 25; price, 16
ostriches, 21, 24
oxen, **14**, **40**

Papua New Guinea, **15**
peanuts. *See* groundnuts
pest control, 16, 22, 37, 39
pigeons, 24
pigs, **21**, 28–30, **29**, **30**, **35**, 39

pineapples, 11, **17**
plantains, 15
plowing, **40**
plums, **6**
pollination, 41
popcorn, 13
potatoes, 10
poultry, **18–19**, **20**, 21–25: exotic,
   21, 25; feed for, 24–25, 39;
   heritage varieties, 35; housing,
   18, **19**, 23, **24**, 25. *See also*
   chickens, ducks, eggs, emus,
   geese, ostriches, pigeons,
   turkeys
pumpkins, **9**, 10: seeds, **9**

rabbits, 32
Rare Breeds Canada, 35
rice, 14, 15: planting, **14**, **40**
roti, **13**

sacred plants, 15
savannah, African, 14
schools, gardens, 6, 12
seed banks, **10–11**
seeds, 8–11, **8**, **9**: preserving, 10–11;
   seedless plants, 11; sprouts, 9
sheep, 32–34, **32**, **33**, **34**, 35
sorghum, **14**
South America, 13, 15
soybeans, 15, **16**
sprouts, **9**
staple crops, 12–15
strawberries, 11
sugarcane, 40
Sustainable Harvest International,
   11
Svalbard Global Seed Vault, **11**
sweet potatoes, 15

taro, 15
tofu, 15
tomatoes, **6**
transportation, 38, **38**, **39**, **42**
turkeys, **23**, 24
Tyrannosaurus rex, 21

urban farms, 6, 8, **12**, 18, 25

volunteers, supporting farmers, **11**

water buffalo, **38**
wheat, **12**, 14, 15
wool, 32, **33**
words, referring to animals, 23,
   26, 28, 33, 34
worms, **41**

yams, **15**